Sanjeev Kapoor

Vegetarian Soups

In association with Alyona Kapoor

Popular Prakashan
www.popularprakashan.com

Published by
POPULAR PRAKASHAN PVT. LTD.
301, Mahalaxmi Chambers
22, Bhulabhai Desai Road
Mumbai - 400 026
for Khana Khazana Publications Pvt. Ltd.

First Published 2010
Fourth Reprint 2014

(4095)
ISBN: 978-81-7991-347-5

Design: Anjali Sawant
Photography: Alim Bolar, Bharat Bhirangi, Dilip Yande, Mangesh Parab,
Mukesh Munim, Satish Parab, Swapnil Naik

PRINTED IN INDIA
by Saurabh Printers Pvt. Ltd.
A-16, Sector 4, Noida

Author's Note

Nutritious, delicious and easy to make, a soup is no longer just the commencement of a meal, but a meal in itself.

Homemade vegetable soups are packed with antioxidants; contain fewer calories and are filling too, without artificial additives. Soups are as nutritious to consume, as they are quick to make!

Find out how with my selection of Indian and international soups. Stir up a royal Badam ka Shorba, or the classic French Onion and Garlic Soup. Try the delicious Italian Mushroom Soup, or enjoy the comforting warmth of the Vegetable Noodle Soup.

Try them, and I assure you they will become an integral part of your meals.

Happy cooking!

Contents

Badam Ka Shorba

175 grams almonds
2 teaspoons butter
1¼ teaspoons refined flour
1 cup milk
½ teaspoon sugar
Salt to taste
¼ teaspoon white pepper powder
1½ tablespoons cream

- Soak the almonds in hot water for a few minutes. Drain and peel. Slice ten or twelve almonds for garnishing and grind the rest to a smooth paste.
- Melt the butter in a non-stick pan; add the flour and sauté for one minute. Gradually pour in the milk, stirring continuously to prevent lumps from forming. Add the sugar, salt and white pepper powder and cook, stirring continuously, till the mixture comes to a boil.
- Lower the heat and simmer for five minutes, stirring occasionally. Add the almond paste and two cups of hot water and simmer for ten to fifteen minutes, stirring occasionally, till the soup thickens.
- Toast the sliced almonds. Sprinkle the toasted almonds and drizzle the cream over the soup just before serving piping hot.

Badam ka Shorba

Curried Cauliflower Soup

1 medium cauliflower, separated into small florets

1 medium potato, cut into small pieces

1½ teaspoons oil

1 medium onion, finely chopped

½ inch ginger, finely chopped

4 garlic cloves, finely chopped

4 cups Vegetable Stock (page 95)

½ teaspoon cumin seeds

¼ teaspoon mustard seeds

½ teaspoon turmeric powder

2 teaspoons coriander powder

1 cup yogurt

½ cup milk

2 teaspoons gram flour

Salt to taste

A few sprigs of fresh coriander, chopped

- Soak the cauliflower and potato in salted water. Drain.
- Heat one teaspoon oil in a non-stick pan; add the chopped onion and sauté for two minutes. Add the chopped ginger and garlic, and sauté

for another two minutes. Add the drained potato and cauliflower, and stir on high heat for three to four minutes.

- Stir in two cups of vegetable stock and bring to a boil. Cover and simmer till the cauliflower and the potato are cooked. Remove from the heat and cool the mixture. Purée the cauliflower and potato mixture in a blender.
- Heat the remaining oil and add the cumin seeds and mustard seeds. When the mustard seeds start to splutter, add the cauliflower and potato purée along with the remaining vegetable stock. Mix well and cook on low heat. Add the turmeric powder and coriander powder, and mix well.
- Whisk the yogurt and milk in a bowl. Add the gram flour and continue to whisk till smooth. Stir the mixture into the soup and cook for a while. Season with salt if required. Serve hot, garnished with the chopped coriander.

Chef's Tip

A leftover dish made of potatoes and cauliflower can be puréed and used to make the soup.

Matar Ka Shorba

500 gram green peas, shelled, boiled and puréed
2 inches ginger, chopped
8-10 garlic cloves
2 green chillies, chopped
3 tablespoons ghee or oil

½ teaspoon cumin seeds
2 bay leaves
1 medium onion, finely chopped
Salt to taste
¼ cup cream

- Grind together the ginger, garlic and green chillies to a paste.
- Heat the ghee or oil in a non-stick pan; add the cumin seeds and bay leaves, and sauté for half a minute.
- Add the chopped onion and sauté till it turns light pink. Add the ginger-garlic-green chilli paste and sauté for a while.
- Add the green pea purée and cook for five minutes, stirring continuously. Stir in three cups of water and bring to a boil.

Matar ka Shorba

- Season with salt and stir. Remove the bay leaves and discard. Lower the heat and cook for another five minutes till the soup reaches the desired consistency.
- Stir in most of the cream and serve hot, garnished with a swirl of the remaining cream.

Corn And Spinach Soup

2 cups corn kernels, boiled

1 kilogram spinach, blanched and puréed

2 teaspoons oil

5 green chillies, chopped

6-8 garlic cloves, chopped

Salt to taste

½ teaspoon *garam masala* powder

½ tablespoon lemon juice

4 tablespoons fresh cream

- Heat the oil in a non-stick pan; add the green chillies and garlic, and sauté for half a minute.
- Add the spinach purée and salt, and sauté over medium heat for two or three minutes.
- Add the *garam masala* powder and lemon juice, and simmer for one minute.
- Stir in the boiled corn and serve hot, garnished with fresh cream.

Dal Ka Shorba

¾ cup skinless split green gram, soaked

1 teaspoon olive oil

½ medium onion, chopped

1 inch ginger, chopped

3 garlic cloves, chopped

2 green chillies, chopped

½ teaspoon turmeric powder

Salt to taste

½ teaspoon roasted cumin powder

1 tablespoon lemon juice

2 tablespoons chopped fresh coriander

- Heat the olive oil in a deep non-stick pan. Add the onion and sauté for a minute. Add the ginger, garlic and green chillies.
- Sauté on low heat and add the turmeric powder, salt, roasted cumin powder and the drained green gram.
- Add five cups of water, bring to a boil and cook, on medium heat for ten to fifteen minutes, or till the *dal* is very soft. Pass through a soup strainer.
- Bring the strained *dal* to a boil and add water to adjust the consistency. Continue to simmer for two to three minutes. Stir in the lemon juice.
- Serve piping hot, garnished with the chopped coriander.

Microwaved Tamatar Ka Shorba

8 medium tomatoes, quartered

1 tablespoon oil

4-5 black peppercorns

1 large onion, cut into 1-inch pieces

4 garlic cloves, chopped

1 medium carrot, cut into 1-inch pieces

2 tablespoons gram flour

Salt to taste

1 teaspoon red chilli powder

1 teaspoon roasted cumin powder

- Place the tomatoes, oil, peppercorns, onion, garlic, carrot, gram flour, salt, chilli powder and the cumin powder into a deep microwave-safe bowl and cook, covered, for fifteen minutes on HIGH (100%).
- Set aside to cool. When cool, purée in a blender till smooth.
- Add one and a half cups of water and cook on HIGH (100%) for five minutes. Serve piping hot.

Microwaved Tamatar ka Shorba

Microwaved Palak Ka Shorba

30 spinach leaves, roughly chopped

2-3 cloves

½ inch cinnamon

2 teaspoons oil

1 inch ginger, chopped

2 garlic cloves, chopped

2 green chillies, chopped

1 small onion, chopped

Salt to taste

4 cups Vegetable Stock (page 95)

1 tablespoon lemon juice

½ teaspoon roasted cumin powder

- Tie the cloves and cinnamon in a piece of muslin to make a *potli.*
- Place the oil, ginger, garlic, green chillies and onion into a large microwave-safe bowl and cook for five minutes on HIGH (100%).
- Add the spinach, salt, vegetable stock and *garam masala potli*. Cook, covered, on HIGH (100%) for five minutes.
- Remove the *masala potli* and set the mixture aside to cool slightly. Purée the spinach mixture in a blender till smooth.
- Stir in the lemon juice and sprinkle with the roasted cumin powder. Heat just before serving.

Red Pumpkin Soup

1 kilogram red pumpkin, diced

4 tablespoons butter

3 bay leaves

15-20 black peppercorns

3 large onions, sliced

Salt to taste

1 teaspoon white pepper powder

1 tablespoon lemon juice

½ cup fresh cream

- Heat the butter in a pressure cooker; add the bay leaves, peppercorns and onions, and sauté for two minutes.
- Add the diced pumpkin and sauté for half a minute. Add four cups water and cook under pressure until pressure is released once (one whistle).
- Strain and reserve the stock. Remove the bay leaves. Purée the vegetables. Add the reserved stock and one cup of water to the purée.
- Add the salt and white pepper powder, and bring to a boil. Stir in the lemon juice. Serve hot, garnished with the fresh cream.

Note: *This soup can be served in the shells of scooped out small red pumpkins.*

Red Pumpkin Soup

Pepper Rasam

10-12 peppercorns, coarsely powdered

3 tablespoons split pigeon peas

1 teaspoon split Bengal gram

1 teaspoon skinless split black gram

6-7 dried red chillies

¼ teaspoon fenugreek seeds

½ teaspoon cumin seeds

¾ teaspoon mustard seeds

1 teaspoon coriander seeds

1 tablespoon oil

3 garlic cloves, crushed

10 curry leaves

Salt to taste

¼ teaspoon turmeric powder

2 tablespoons Tamarind Pulp (page 95)

1 tablespoon jaggery, grated

Seasoning

1 tablespoon oil

½ teaspoon mustard seeds

2 dried red chillies

¼ teaspoon asafoetida

10 curry leaves

- Soak the pigeon peas in one cup of water for half an hour and pressure-cook in one cup of water. Mash well and set aside.
- Dry-roast and powder the split Bengal gram, split black gram, red chillies, fenugreek seeds, cumin seeds, half a teaspoon of mustard seeds and coriander seeds.
- Heat the oil in a non-stick *kadai* and add the garlic, remaining mustard seeds, crushed peppercorns and curry leaves.
- When the mustard starts to splutter, add the mashed *dal*, the *masala* powder mixed with a little water, salt, turmeric powder, tamarind pulp and jaggery. Mix well and stir in five cups of water.
- Bring the mixture to a boil, lower the heat and simmer for ten to fifteen minutes. Strain the soup through a piece of muslin.
- For the seasoning, heat the oil in a non-stick pan. Add the mustard seeds, and when they start to splutter, add the red chillies, asafoetida and curry leaves. Pour over the *rasam*. Serve hot.

Vegetable Clear Soup

6-8 fresh button mushrooms, sliced

½ medium carrot, thinly sliced

4-6 Chinese cabbage leaves, cut into 1-inch pieces

1 inch celery stalk, diagonally sliced

1 spring onion, sliced

1 medium red capsicum, seeded and cut into 1-inch pieces

8-10 snow peas, halved

12-16 spinach leaves, chopped

4-5 cups Vegetable Stock (page 95)

2-3 garlic cloves, crushed

¼ teaspoon MSG (optional)

¼ teaspoon peppercorns, crushed

½ cup bean sprouts

Salt to taste

½ teaspoon lemon juice (optional)

- Heat the vegetable stock in a non-stick pan, add the garlic and bring to a boil. Add the mushrooms, carrot, Chinese cabbage, celery, spring onion, red capsicum, snow peas, and spinach, and cook for two to three minutes.
- Add the MSG, peppercorns, bean sprouts and salt to taste Stir in the lemon juice and serve piping hot.

Sabzi Ka Shorba

3 medium potatoes, cut into ½-inch cubes

3 large tomatoes, chopped

100 grams bottle gourd, cut into ½-inch cubes

2 tablespoons oil

5-6 black peppercorns

2 cloves

2 onions, chopped

2 garlic cloves, crushed

1 inch ginger, chopped

3 cups Vegetable Stock (page 95)

¼ teaspoon turmeric powder

Salt to taste

½ teaspoon sugar

½ teaspoon black pepper powder

1 tablespoon lemon juice

1 spring onion, chopped

- Heat the oil in a deep non-stick pan; add the peppercorns and cloves, and sauté for half a minute. Add the onions and cook over medium heat till translucent.
- Add the garlic and ginger, and stir. Add the potatoes, tomatoes and bottle gourd, and cook over medium heat for five minutes, stirring occasionally.

- Add the vegetable stock, turmeric powder, salt, sugar and pepper powder. Increase the heat and bring the soup to a boil.
- Lower the heat and simmer for about thirty minutes, or till the vegetables are tender. Cool and purée in a blender. Pass the purée through a strainer.
- Return the purée to the pan, add the lemon juice, and bring the soup to a boil. Serve hot, garnished with the chopped spring onion.

Sabzi ka Shorba

Tomato And Paneer Soup

5 medium tomatoes, chopped

100 grams cottage cheese, cut into ¾-inch cubes

2 teaspoons oil

1 medium onion, chopped

1 inch ginger, chopped

4 garlic cloves, chopped

1-2 green chillies, chopped

4 tablespoons tomato ketchup

4 cups Vegetable Stock (page 95)

Salt to taste

¼ teaspoon crushed black peppercorns

½ tablespoon rice flour

A few sprigs of fresh coriander, chopped

- Heat the oil in a large non-stick pan; add the chopped onion and sauté on high heat. Add the ginger and garlic, and sauté for a few seconds.
- Add the tomatoes, and green chillies, and sauté for a minute. Add the tomato ketchup and vegetable stock and bring the mixture to a boil.
- Remove from heat and strain. Reserve the stock. Purée the vegetables and add it to the strained stock.

- Cook the mixture on medium heat. Season with salt and the crushed peppercorns.
- Mix the rice flour in half a cup of water to make a smooth paste.
- Add the cottage cheese cubes and the rice flour paste to the boiling soup to thicken it. Cook for a minute.
- Serve piping hot, garnished with the chopped coriander.

Tomato Paruppu Rasam

2 medium tomatoes, chopped

4 tablespoons split pigeon peas

1½ teaspoons *rasam* powder

½ lemon-sized ball tamarind

¼ cup chopped fresh coriander

¼ teaspoon asafoetida

Salt to taste

10-12 curry leaves

4 tablespoons pure ghee

½ teaspoon mustard seeds

2 dried red chillies

- Cook the split pigeon peas in two cups of water until soft. Strain and mash well. Reserve the strained cooking liquid.
- Soak the tamarind in one cup of warm water; squeeze out the pulp, strain and reserve.
- Reserve some chopped coriander for garnishing. Mix the tamarind pulp with the remaining chopped coriander, *rasam* powder, asafoetida, salt and half the curry leaves.

Tomato Paruppu Rasam

- Bring to a boil, lower the heat and simmer for two to three minutes.
- Add the chopped tomatoes and reserved cooking liquid. Simmer for four to five minutes and stir in the mashed *dal*. Stir well and cook for one minute longer.
- Remove from the heat and sprinkle the reserved chopped coriander.
- Heat the ghee in a small non-stick pan; add the mustard seeds and sauté till they begin to splutter. Add the red chillies and remaining curry leaves, and stir well.
- Pour the sizzling spices over the *rasam* and cover immediately to trap the flavours. Serve hot.

Chef's Tips

- To serve the *rasam* as an appetiser, strain and pour into small glasses, garnished with a slice of lemon.
- Traditionally, *rasam* is cooked in a pan made from a special alloy, which gives the *rasam* its unique flavour.

Chilled Cucumber And Buttermilk Soup

2 medium cucumbers, seeded and roughly chopped

2 cups buttermilk

A few sprigs of mint

½ inch ginger, roughly chopped

1 green chilli, seeded and chopped

2 teaspoons lemon juice

Salt to taste

½ teaspoon black pepper powder

- Reserve a few mint sprigs for garnishing, and finely chop the rest.
- Place the cucumbers, ginger, green chilli and the lemon juice in a blender and blend till smooth.
- Stir in the buttermilk and chopped mint. Season the mixture with the salt and freshly ground pepper.
- Garnish with the mint and serve chilled.

Chef's Tip

If you do not have buttermilk, you can mix equal quantities of curd and water, and whisk till smooth.

Chilled Musk Melon Soup

1 kilogram musk melon, seeded and cut into 1-inch pieces

A few sprigs of mint

1 inch ginger, roughly chopped

¼ cup skimmed milk yogurt

3 tablespoons lemon juice

Salt to taste

¼ teaspoon pepper powder

2 cups crushed ice

- Reserve a sprig of the mint for garnishing.
- In a blender, purée together, the musk melon, mint and ginger. Add the yogurt, lemon juice and crushed ice, and blend for a few minutes longer.
- Season with the salt and pepper powder. Serve chilled, garnished with a sprig of mint.

Chef's Tips

- The consistency of this soup should be very thick, however, if you prefer, you may thin it down by adding a half a cup of chilled milk.
- Go easy on the mint leaves as too much mint flavour and taste can be over powering.

Minted Green Pea Soup

10-12 fresh mint leaves

1 cup shelled green peas

1 tablespoon butter

1 small onion, finely chopped

2-3 garlic cloves, finely chopped

3 cups Vegetable Stock (page 95)

1 small potato, sliced

1 cup milk

Salt to taste

¼ teaspoon white pepper powder

½ cup cream

- Heat the butter in a non-stick pan; add the onion and garlic, and sauté till the onion turns translucent.
- Add the vegetable stock, potato slices and mint leaves, reserving a few leaves for garnishing. Bring to a boil and add the green peas. Boil for five to seven minutes, uncovered, on high heat.
- When the vegetables soften, remove from heat, cool and strain. Reserve the stock. Purée the peas and other vegetables using a little stock, if required.

- Mix the purée with the reserved stock and milk, and bring to a boil. Add the salt and white pepper powder.
- Stir in the cream and serve, garnished with the remaining mint leaves.

Minted Green Pea Soup

Broccoli Soup

2 small pieces of broccoli, separated into florets

1 medium onion, finely chopped

2-3 garlic cloves, finely chopped

2 tablespoons butter

1 tablespoon oil

1 tablespoon refined flour

2½ cups Vegetable Stock (page 95)

1 cup milk

Salt to taste

¼ teaspoon white pepper powder

½ cup cream

- Blanch four broccoli florets and reserve for garnishing.
- Melt the butter in a non-stick pan on medium heat. Add the oil to prevent the butter from burning.
- Add the chopped onion and garlic, and sauté till the onion turns translucent. Add the flour and sauté for a minute. Add the broccoli and cook for two to three minutes.
- Add the stock, bring it to a boil and cook for five minutes on high heat without covering the pan.

- Strain and cool the broccoli. Reserve the stock. Pass the broccoli through a sieve or process in a blender. Mix it with the strained stock and milk in a non-stick pan.
- Place the pan back on high heat; bring to a boil and season with salt and the white pepper powder.
- Stir in the cream, simmer for two to three minutes and serve hot, garnished with the blanched broccoli florets.

Green Gram And Cottage Cheese Broth

½ cup whole green gram

100 grams cottage cheese, cut into ½-inch cubes

Salt to taste

1 tablespoon oil

½ teaspoon cumin seeds

2-3 spring onions, chopped

1 inch ginger, chopped

3 green chillies, chopped

1½ tablespoons lemon juice

1 cup boiled eggless noodles, deep-fried

- Pressure-cook the green gram along with two cups of water and salt till done. Cool and process in a blender to a smooth purée.
- Strain and add four to five cups of water and stir to make a thin broth.
- Heat the oil in a non-stick pan; add the cumin seeds and when they begin to change colour, add the spring onions and ginger, and sauté over medium heat for half a minute.

- Add the green chillies and continue to sauté for half a minute longer. Add the green gram broth and bring to a boil. Lower the heat, add the lemon juice, adjust the seasoning and simmer, uncovered, for five minutes.
- Stir in the cottage cheese and simmer for half a minute.
- Ladle the soup into individual serving bowls, garnish with the fried noodles and serve hot.

Minestrone

4 medium tomatoes

1½ tablespoons olive oil

6-8 garlic cloves, chopped

1 medium onion, chopped

1 medium carrot, cut into ½-inch cubes

½ leek, cut into ½-inch pieces

1 celery stalk, cut into ½-inch pieces

3-4 French beans, cut into ½-inch pieces

1 medium zucchini, cut into ½-inch cubes

1 medium potato, cut into ½-inch cubes

¼ cup shelled green peas

½ cup tomato purée

10-12 fresh basil leaves

3 cups Vegetable Stock (page 95)

2 tablespoons macaroni

Salt to taste

½ teaspoon white pepper powder

½ cup grated Parmesan cheese

Minestrone

- Score the base of the tomatoes. Blanch the tomatoes in plenty of hot water for two minutes and transfer them immediately to a bowl of cold water. Peel the skin, cut into half and remove the seeds. Cut the flesh into half-inch pieces.
- Heat the olive oil in a large non-stick pan; add the garlic, onion, carrot, leek and celery, and cook, stirring occasionally, for about five minutes.
- Add the French beans, zucchini, potato, green peas, tomato purée and tomatoes. Tear half the basil leaves roughly and add to the pan with the vegetable stock; cook for eight minutes. Add the macaroni, salt and pepper powder, cover and cook for five minutes.
- Cut the remaining basil leaves into strips and sprinkle over the soup. Sprinkle the Parmesan cheese and serve piping hot.

Chef's Tip

You may use spring onions instead of leeks.

Healthy Tomato And Green Gram Soup

4 medium tomatoes, quartered

2 tablespoons skinless split green gram, soaked and drained

1 tablespoon olive oil

1 small onion, sliced

1 inch ginger, sliced

2 garlic cloves, sliced

Salt to taste

1 tablespoon sugar

White pepper powder to taste

4 brown bread slices

4 fresh coriander sprigs

- Heat the oil in a pressure cooker. Add the onion, ginger and garlic, and sauté till lightly browned.
- Add the split green gram and sauté for a minute. Add two cups of water and bring the mixture to a boil. Add the salt, sugar and white pepper powder, and stir. Add the tomatoes and mix.
- Cover the cooker with the lid and cook under pressure till the pressure is released four times (four whistles).

- Cut the brown bread slices into heart shapes with a cookie cutter. Heat a non-stick pan and toast the bread hearts till crisp and golden brown.
- Strain the cooked tomato-gram mixture and reserve the stock. Blend the solids in a blender to make a smooth purée.
- Pass the purée through a sieve into a deep non-stick pan. Stir in the strained stock and bring the mixture to a boil. Adjust the seasoning.
- Pour the soup into four soup bowls, garnish with the bread hearts and fresh coriander sprigs, and serve hot.

Healthy Tomato and Green Gram Soup

Cottage Cheese And Lemon Grass Soup

200 grams cottage cheese, cut into ½-inch cubes

1 inch lemon grass, chopped

1 teaspoon oil

3 garlic cloves, chopped

4-5 cups Vegetable Stock (page 95)

1 fresh red chilli, sliced

Salt to taste

A pinch of MSG (optional)

½ tablespoon lemon juice

2-3 spring onion green stalks, sliced

- Heat the oil in a non-stick pan; add the garlic and sauté over medium heat for half a minute.
- Add the lemon grass and continue to sauté for half a minute. Add the vegetable stock and bring to a boil.
- Lower the heat, add the red chilli, salt and MSG, and simmer, uncovered, for five minutes, stirring occasionally. Add the cottage cheese and lemon juice, stir and continue to simmer for one minute.
- Ladle the soup into individual serving bowls, garnish with the spring onion greens and serve hot.

Tomato And Fresh Basil Soup

10-15 medium tomatoes, chopped

2 tablespoons shredded fresh basil + a few leaves, for garnishing

1 tablespoon olive oil

2 tablespoons butter

1 medium onion, chopped

3 garlic cloves, chopped

4 cups Vegetable Stock (page 95)

Salt to taste

10-12 black peppercorns, freshly ground

⅓ cup double cream

3-4 sundried tomatoes, soaked and cut into strips

- Heat the oil and butter in a large non-stick pan; add the onion and cook gently for five minutes, stirring frequently, until soft, but not brown.
- Add the tomatoes, garlic and vegetable stock. Season with salt and the freshly ground peppercorns. Bring to a boil, lower heat and simmer gently, partially covered, for twenty minutes. Set aside to cool.

- Add the shredded basil and purée the mixture in a blender. Strain the purée into a fresh non-stick pan.
- Add more stock if the purée is too thick and adjust the seasoning.
- Add the cream and cook over low heat for two minutes, making sure the soup does not boil.
- Serve hot, garnished with the fresh basil and sun-dried tomato strips.

Tomato and Fresh Basil Soup

French Onion And Garlic Soup

3 medium onions, thinly sliced

5-6 garlic cloves

4 slices brown bread, cut into small round slices

2 tablespoons olive oil

1 medium carrot, thinly sliced

4 cups Vegetable Stock (page 95)

Salt to taste

¼ teaspoon white pepper powder

¼ cup grated cheese

- Chop three to four garlic cloves and set the rest aside.
- Spread one tablespoon of the olive oil over the bread rounds and rub with the whole garlic cloves. Toast the slices in an oven till crisp.
- Heat the remaining olive oil in a non-stick pan and sauté the onions on medium heat till brown. Set aside a few fried onions for garnishing.
- Add the chopped garlic to the onions in the pan and sauté till light brown. Add the carrot and sauté for few minutes.

- Add the vegetable stock and bring to a boil. Lower the heat and let it simmer for ten to fifteen minutes. Add the salt and pepper powder.
- To serve, ladle the soup into individual bowls and float the toasted brown bread on top.
- Sprinkle with the grated cheese and fried brown onions, and serve hot.

Mushroom Soup With Light Soy Sauce

30 grams fresh button mushrooms
1 teaspoon light soy sauce
3 cups Vegetable Stock (page 95)
150 grams silken bean curd, finely diced
Salt to taste
½ teaspoon black pepper powder
4 teaspoons sliced spring onions

- Pour the vegetable stock and light soy sauce into a deep non-stick pan and bring the mixture to a boil.
- Add the mushrooms and bean curd and cook over low heat for three to four minutes, but do not allow the mixture to boil. Add the salt and pepper powder. Stir to mix well.
- Ladle the soup into individual soup bowls, garnish with a teaspoon of spring onions on top, and serve piping hot.

Mushroom Soup with Light Soy Sauce

Microwaved Garden Vegetables And Almond Soup

¼ small head of broccoli, separated into medium florets

5-6 fresh mushrooms, sliced

1 medium carrot, cut into ½-inch cubes

2 spring onions, chopped

¼ cup sweetcorn kernels

3-4 lettuce leaves, shredded

20-25 almonds

1 tablespoon oil

3 garlic cloves, chopped

4 cups Vegetable Stock (page 95)

Salt to taste

A pinch of thyme

4 fresh basil leaves, shredded

1 teaspoon soy sauce

- Chop the spring onion bulbs and four to five greens.
- Place the almonds with sufficient water in a deep bowl and cook on HIGH (100%), for three minutes. Drain, peel and cut into slivers and set aside.

- Place the oil, carrot, spring onions, corn kernels, almond slivers, garlic, vegetable stock and salt in a microwave-safe dish and cook, on HIGH (100%), for seven minutes.
- Add the broccoli, mushrooms, spring onion greens, lettuce, thyme, basil, and soy sauce, and cook on HIGH (100%) for five minutes.
- Serve piping hot.

Gazpacho

6 medium tomatoes, quartered
2-3 slices white bread
3-4 garlic cloves, coarsely chopped
1 medium cucumber, seeded and roughly chopped
1 medium green capsicum, roughly chopped
Salt to taste
2 tablespoons wine vinegar
½ cup olive oil

Garnish

1 small onion, chopped
1 small green capsicum, chopped
1 slice white bread, cut into ½-inch cubes

- Soak the bread slices in half a cup of water for five minutes and squeeze out the excess water.
- Process the bread with the garlic, tomatoes, cucumber and chilled water in a blender. Add the capsicum and salt, and process again. Add the wine vinegar and olive oil, and continue to blend.
- Strain the soup into a bowl and chill in a refrigerator. Garnish with the onion, capsicum and bread cubes, and serve chilled.

Chef's Tip

You can use malt vinegar or lemon juice instead of wine vinegar.

Vegetable Noodle Soup

4-5 fresh button mushrooms, finely sliced

1 medium carrot, grated

½ medium green capsicum, cut into thin strips

8-10 spinach leaves, finely shredded

40 grams eggless noodles

1 tablespoon oil

2-3 garlic cloves, crushed

1 dried red chilli, seeded and finely chopped

4-5 cups Vegetable Stock (page 95)

¼ teaspoon MSG (optional)

¼ teaspoon white pepper powder

Salt to taste

1 tablespoon white vinegar

- Heat the oil in a non-stick pan; add the garlic and stir-fry for half a minute. Add the mushrooms, carrot and capsicum, and stir-fry for two minutes.
- Add the red chilli and immediately stir in the stock.

- Bring the mixture to a boil and add the noodles; lower the heat and simmer for three to four minutes, stirring occasionally.
- Add the MSG, white pepper powder and salt to taste.
- Stir in the vinegar and shredded spinach, cook for one minute and serve hot.

Chef's Tip

Vary the quantity of noodles to taste. To make a complete meal of this soup, increase the quantity of noodles and serve in a large bowl.

Vegetable Noodle Soup

Lemon Pepper Soup

1½ tablespoons lemon juice
3 black peppercorns, crushed
¾ teaspoon oil
¾ tablespoon gram flour
¾ medium carrot, grated
¼ small cabbage, finely shredded
4 fresh button mushrooms, sliced
½ medium green capsicum, chopped
½ medium tomato, finely chopped
Salt to taste
3-4 cups Vegetable Stock (page 95)
½ cup bean sprouts

- Heat the oil in a non-stick pan; add the gram flour and stir-fry for a few seconds.
- Add the carrot, cabbage and mushrooms, and stir to mix. Add the capsicum, tomato and salt, and stir-fry for one minute.
- Add the vegetable stock and bring to a boil; simmer for two to three minutes. Add the crushed peppercorns and remove from the heat.
- Stir in the bean sprouts and the lemon juice, and serve piping hot.

Oriental Mixed Vegetable Soup

¼ medium Chinese cabbage, shredded

¼ small cauliflower, coarsely chopped

4 one-inch celery pieces, chopped

100 grams bean curd, cut into ½-inch cubes

2 tablespoons oil

2 garlic cloves, crushed

1 fresh red chilli, sliced

5-6 cups Vegetable Stock (page 95)

Salt to taste

¼ teaspoon white pepper powder

1 teaspoon brown sugar

1 tablespoon light soy sauce

2 tablespoons chopped fresh coriander

- Heat the oil in a non-stick pan; add the garlic and fresh red chilli, and sauté for half a minute. Add the cabbage, cauliflower and celery, and sauté for another minute.
- Add the vegetable stock and bring to a boil. Lower the heat; add the salt, white pepper powder, brown sugar and soy sauce.
- Simmer for five or six minutes, or until the vegetables are tender. Add the bean curd and chopped coriander and serve hot.

Mushroom Soup With Chillies

20-25 fresh button mushrooms, quartered

1 tablespoon oil

4 cups Vegetable Stock (page 95)

Salt to taste

1 inch ginger, cut into strips

¼ cup chopped fresh coriander

4-5 spring onion green stalks, chopped

Chilli Paste

4 dried red chillies, halved

1 tablespoon oil

4 shallots, chopped

3 garlic cloves, chopped

1 inch galangal, sliced

- For the chilli paste, heat the oil in a non-stick pan; add the dried chillies, shallots, garlic and galangal, and sauté for four to five minutes. Cool and grind to a fine paste.
- For the soup, heat one tablespoon of oil in a separate non-stick pan; add the mushrooms and sauté for one minute. Transfer the

mushrooms to a plate. To the same pan, add the vegetable stock and bring to a boil.

- Add the salt, sautéed mushrooms and ginger strips. Stir in the chilli paste and simmer for five minutes.
- Sprinkle the chopped coriander and spring onion greens over the soup and serve hot.

Roasted Pumpkin And Walnut Soup

1 (700 grams) small red pumpkin, halved and seeded

8 walnut kernels, roughly chopped

1 tablespoon oil

2 tablespoons butter

1 large onion, finely chopped

4 cups Vegetable Stock (page 95)

1 teaspoon curry powder

½ cup fresh cream

Salt to taste

¼ teaspoon white pepper powder

1 tablespoon lemon juice

2 tablespoons fresh parsley, finely chopped

- Smear the oil over the pumpkin and roast in a preheated oven at 200°C/400°F/Gas Mark 6, for half an hour. Alternatively, peel and cut into cubes and sauté with the onion as described below.
- Remove the roasted pumpkin from the oven and leave to cool. Peel and cut into cubes.
- Heat the butter in a non-stick pan and add the chopped onion and sauté till translucent.

Roasted Pumpkin and Walnut Soup

- Add the pumpkin cubes, walnuts and half the stock, and cook for five minutes. Take off the heat, cool and purée the pumpkin mixture.
- Transfer the purée to a non-stick pan. Add the remaining stock to the purée and place the pan back on the heat. Add the curry powder and bring to a boil. Lower heat, add the cream and simmer for a few seconds.
- Season with the salt, white pepper powder and lemon juice.
- Serve, garnished with the chopped parsley.

Southern Italian Vegetable Soup

2 medium tomatoes
1 medium carrot, finely chopped
2 medium potatoes, finely diced
¼ small cabbage, finely diced
6-8 fresh basil leaves
1 teaspoon olive oil
1 medium onion, finely chopped
4 garlic cloves, finely chopped
1-inch celery stalk, chopped
Salt to taste
White pepper powder to taste
¼ cup macaroni
4 cups Vegetable Stock (page 95)

- Score the base of the tomatoes and make a small incision at the bottom. Boil one cup of water and blanch the tomatoes for one minute and remove immediately. Peel, remove seeds and purée the tomatoes.
- Reserve a few basil leaves for garnishing and chop the rest.

- Heat the olive oil in a non-stick pan; add the onion and garlic, and sauté till they turn translucent.
- Add the celery, carrot and potatoes. Cook for five minutes, stirring continuously.
- Add the cabbage, puréed tomatoes, salt, white pepper powder, basil, macaroni and four cups of the stock or water, and bring to a boil.
- Lower the heat and simmer till vegetables are cooked and the soup has thickened.
- Garnish with the fresh basil and serve hot.

Thai Hot And Sour Vegetable Soup

8-10 snow peas, sliced diagonally

5-6 straw mushrooms, halved

¼ small cabbage, cut into ½-inch cubes

1-inch bamboo shoot

2 lemon grass stalks, sliced

4 Kaffir lime leaves

1 tablespoon Red Curry Paste (page 95)

1 tablespoon oil

Salt to taste

4 fresh red chillies, sliced diagonally

2 tablespoons lemon juice

2 fresh coriander sprigs, roughly torn

- Heat the oil in a non-stick pan.
- Add the snow peas, straw mushrooms, bamboo shoot and lemon grass, and toss to mix. Bruise the lime leaves; add to the pan and mix.

- Stir in the red curry paste. Add four cups of water and bring the mixture to a boil; add the cabbage and salt. Stir again and add the fresh red chillies.
- Remove from the heat and add the lemon juice. Add the coriander leaves, stir and serve piping hot.

Chef's Tip

Add a little coconut milk for a milder flavour.

Toasted Almond And Spinach Soup

¼ cup almonds, toasted and slivered

400 grams spinach, shredded

1 tablespoon oil

1 bay leaf

1 medium onion, chopped

5 garlic cloves, chopped

6-8 black peppercorns

Salt to taste

1 cup milk

- Heat the oil in a non-stick pan; add the bay leaf, onion, garlic and peppercorns, and sauté for a few seconds.
- Reserve a little spinach, and add the rest to the pan. Sauté for four to five minutes.
- Add three cups of water and salt. Bring the mixture to a boil and cook for a minute longer.
- Take the pan off the heat and strain the mixture. Reserve the cooking liquid. When slightly cooled, remove and discard the bay leaf and purée the spinach in a blender.

- Transfer the purée to a non-stick pan; add the reserved cooking liquid and mix. Add the milk, adjust the seasoning and bring the mixture to a boil.
- Place the reserved shredded spinach in individual soup bowls and pour the hot soup over.
- Garnish with almond slivers and serve immediately.

Sweetcorn Soup With Mixed Vegetables And Bean Curd

150 grams cream-style sweetcorn

½ cup sweetcorn kernels

¼ small cabbage, chopped

¼ medium carrot, chopped

100 grams bean curd (tofu), cut into ½-inch pieces

2 tablespoons oil

4-5 cups Vegetable Stock (page 95)

Salt to taste

¼ teaspoon white pepper powder

½ tablespoon sugar

¼ teaspoon MSG (optional)

3 tablespoons cornflour

1 spring onion green stalk, chopped

- Heat the oil in a non-stick wok; add the corn, cabbage and carrot, and stir-fry for two minutes. Stir in the vegetable stock and bring to a boil.
- Mix in the cream-style corn and continue to cook for two to three minutes.

- Add the salt, white pepper powder, sugar and MSG. Add the bean curd and stir in the cornflour, mixed with half a cup of water. Cook over a high heat, stirring continuously, for one minute, or until the soup thickens.
- Serve piping hot, garnished with spring onion green.

Sweetcorn Soup with Mixed Vegetables and Bean Curd

Tomato Soup

10-12 medium tomatoes, quartered
2 slices bread, cut into cubes
1 teaspoon sugar
¼ cup cream
½ tablespoon oil
1 tablespoon butter
1 bay leaf
8-10 black peppercorns
1 medium onion, sliced
4 garlic cloves, chopped
2-inch celery stalk, chopped
½ medium carrot, sliced
Salt to taste
1 tablespoon chopped fresh parsley

- Toast the bread cubes in an oven or non-stick frying pan to make croutons.
- Mix together the sugar and cream.
- Heat the oil and butter in a pressure cooker; add the bay leaf, four or five peppercorns and the onion, and sauté until translucent. Add the garlic and celery, and sauté for a few seconds.

- Add the carrot, tomatoes and salt. Sauté for one minute and add three cups of water. Seal the cooker with the lid and cook over medium heat till the pressure is released four or five times (four or five whistles).
- Remove the lid when the pressure has reduced completely, and strain. Reserve the liquid. Remove the peppercorns and bay leaf and discard. Leave the rest of the solids to cool. Purée in a blender till smooth. Pass the purée through a sieve or strainer.
- Add the reserved liquid to the puréed tomatoes and adjust the consistency. Place back on the heat.
- Add the salt, and the remaining peppercorns, and simmer for a couple of minutes.
- Just before serving, stir in the cream and sugar mixture. Serve hot, garnished with the parsley and toasted croutons.

Wonton Soup

16 Wonton Wrappers (page 95)
½ tablespoon oil
2 garlic cloves, chopped
1 spring onion, chopped
½ medium green capsicum, chopped
2-3 French beans, chopped
½ medium carrot, chopped
4-5 cabbage leaves, chopped
¼ teaspoon white pepper powder
Salt to taste
1 teaspoon soy sauce
5-6 cups Vegetable Stock (page 95)
¼ teaspoon MSG (optional)
2 spring onion green stalks, chopped

- For the filling, heat the oil in a non-stick wok; add the garlic and stir-fry for a minute. Add the spring onion, capsicum, French beans, carrot and cabbage, and continue to stir-fry for about two minutes, or until the vegetables are cooked.
- Add half the white pepper powder, salt and soy sauce. Cook over high heat for half a minute. Remove from the heat and cool.

Wonton Soup

- Divide the filling into sixteen equal portions. Place a portion of the filling in the centre of each wonton wrapper, moisten the edges, fold in half diagonally and twist the ends and stick together.
- Heat the stock in a non-stick wok; add the remaining white pepper powder, MSG and salt, and bring to a boil.
- Lower the heat, gently slide in the wontons and simmer for three to four minutes.
- Serve piping hot, garnished with the spring onion greens.

Vegetable Manchow Soup

3-4 fresh button mushrooms, finely chopped

¼ small cabbage, finely chopped

50 grams bean curd, finely chopped

1 medium capsicum, seeded and finely chopped

1 medium carrot, finely diced

2 spring onions, finely chopped

2 tablespoons oil + for deep-frying

1 cup eggless noodles, boiled

½ inch ginger, finely chopped

10-12 garlic cloves, finely chopped

2 green chillies, finely chopped

½ tablespoon red chilli sauce

2 tablespoons dark soy sauce

½ teaspoon white pepper powder

Salt to taste

4-5 cups Vegetable Stock (page 95)

3 tablespoons cornflour

1 tablespoon vinegar

1 spring onion green stalk, finely chopped

- Heat sufficient oil in a non-stick wok and deep-fry the boiled noodles for two to three minutes, or until light brown and crisp. Drain on absorbent paper.

- Heat two tablespoons of oil in a non-stick pan; add the chopped ginger, garlic, and green chillies, and stir-fry for a few seconds. Add the chopped spring onion, and cook for a couple of minutes.
- Add the mushrooms, cabbage, bean curd, capsicum and carrot, and cook on medium heat, stirring continuously for two minutes.
- Add the chilli sauce, soy sauce, white pepper powder and salt to taste, and stir well to mix.
- Stir in the vegetable stock and bring to a boil. Lower the heat and simmer for two to three minutes.
- Mix the cornflour and half a cup of water, stir into the soup and cook for two minutes or until the soup thickens, stirring continuously.
- Stir in the vinegar and serve piping hot, garnished with the crisp fried noodles and spring onion greens.

Cream Of Asparagus And Almond Soup

300 grams asparagus spears
10-12 almonds
Salt to taste
2 tablespoons butter
1 medium onion, chopped
2 tablespoons refined flour
2½ cups vegetable stock
4-5 black peppercorns, crushed
2 cups milk

- Trim the asparagus, discarding the woody part of the stem. Cut the remainder into short lengths, reserving a few tips for garnishing. Blanch the reserved tips in boiling salted water for one or two minutes. Drain and refresh in cold water.
- Blanch the remaining asparagus in boiling water for two to three minutes. Drain and refresh in cold water. Purée in a blender.
- Broil or dry-roast the almonds over medium heat till the skins change colour slightly. Remove from heat, cool and slice into slivers.

- Melt the butter in a non-stick pan and add the onion. Sauté over a low heat until soft. Stir in the flour and cook for one minute, then gradually add the stock and whisk so that no lumps are formed. Bring the mixture to a boil.
- Simmer for two to three minutes until thickened, then stir in the asparagus purée, salt and crushed peppercorns.
- Add the milk and simmer for two to three minutes, stirring continuously.
- Serve hot, garnished with the blanched asparagus tips and almond slivers.

Cream of Asparagus and Almond Soup

Italian Bread Soup

5 slices crusty white bread

1 tablespoon butter

5-6 garlic cloves, chopped

6 cups Vegetable Stock (page 95)

1 teaspoon mixed dried herbs

Salt to taste

5-6 black peppercorns, freshly ground

¼ cup double cream

To Serve

4 slices crusty bread

2 teaspoons olive oil

4 tablespoons grated cheese

- Heat the butter in a large non-stick pan; add the garlic and sauté for a few minutes making sure the garlic does not burn.
- Add the stock. Trim the crusts of the bread slices and add the crusts to the stock.

- Season with the dried herbs, salt and ground peppercorns, and continue to boil for another five minutes. Set aside to cool.
- Purée the mixture in a blender and strain into a clean non-stick pan. Add more stock if the purée is too thick and adjust the seasoning. Bring to a boil.
- Stir in the cream and simmer for two minutes. Do not let the soup boil.
- Preheat the oven to 180°C/350°F/Gas Mark 4.
- Brush both sides of the bread slices with the olive oil and sprinkle the cheese on top. Place on a baking tray and bake till the cheese melts.
- Pour the hot soup into four bowls and place a slice of the cheese toast on top. Serve at once.

Italian Mushroom Soup

5-6 dried chanterelle mushrooms, soaked and cut into strips

25-30 fresh button mushrooms, sliced

6 tablespoons butter

5 garlic cloves, chopped

2 medium onions, sliced

2 tablespoons refined flour

5 cups Vegetable Stock (page 95)

½ teaspoon mixed dried herbs

Salt to taste

5-6 black peppercorns, freshly ground

- Heat one tablespoon of butter in a non-stick pan and add the dried mushrooms strips. Sauté gently over low heat for five minutes. Remove the mushrooms and set aside.
- Add three tablespoons of butter to the same pan. Add the garlic and onions, and sauté for two minutes without browning. Add the button mushrooms and continue to sauté for five more minutes.

- In a separate non-stick pan, heat two tablespoons of butter; add the flour and sauté for two minutes. Add the vegetable stock and stir continuously for two minutes so that no lumps form.
- Add the mushroom-onion mixture and simmer for another five minutes over very low heat. Season with the dried herbs, salt and freshly ground peppercorns. Set aside to cool.
- Purée the mixture in a blender and strain the purée into a clean non-stick pan. Add more stock if the purée is too thick and adjust the seasoning.
- Bring the soup to a boil again. Serve hot, garnished with the sautéed dried mushrooms.

Chef's Tip

Use any dried mushrooms if chanterelle mushrooms are not available.

Balinese Vegetable Soup

225 grams French beans, cut into ½-inch pieces

Salt to taste

2 cups thick Coconut Milk (see below)

1 garlic clove

2 fresh red chillies, chopped

4 almonds

½ tablespoon coriander powder

2 tablespoons oil

1 medium onion, sliced

2 bay leaves

1⅓ cups bean sprouts

2 tablespoons lemon juice

- Cook the French beans in six cups of boiling salted water for three to four minutes. Drain and reserve the cooking liquid.
- Skim off four tablespoons of coconut cream from the top of the coconut milk and reserve.
- Grind the garlic, fresh red chillies, almonds and coriander powder to a paste.

Balinese Vegetable Soup

- Heat the oil in a non-stick wok; add the onion and sauté till translucent. Drain and set aside.
- To the same oil, add the ground paste and sauté without browning for about two minutes. Add the reserved cooking liquid and coconut milk. Bring to a boil and add the bay leaves. Cook, uncovered, for fifteen to twenty minutes.
- Just before serving, add the beans, sautéed onion, bean sprouts, reserved coconut cream and lemon juice. Adjust the salt and serve immediately.

- ***Coconut Milk***

  Process 1 cup grated fresh coconut in a blender with ¼ cup warm water. Pass the ground coconut through a piece of muslin or strainer pressing firmly to extract all the juice, or first milk. Add a ¼ cup of warm water to the strained coconut to get the second, thinner milk from the same solids.

Annexure

- *Red Curry Paste*

  Pound together 10 dried, seeded, soaked and drained long red chillies, a large pinch of salt, 1½ tablespoons chopped galangal, 3 tablespoons chopped lemon grass, 2 teaspoons grated kaffir lime rind, 1 tablespoon chopped fresh coriander roots, 1 tablespoon chopped red shallots and 2 tablespoons chopped garlic with a pestle and mortar, to a smooth paste. Alternatively grind all the ingredients together in a grinder till smooth.

- *Tamarind Pulp*

  Soak 75 grams tamarind in 100 ml warm water for 10-15 minutes. Grind to a smooth paste and strain to remove any fibres. Store in an airtight container in the refrigerator.

- *Vegetable Stock*

  Peel, wash and chop 1 onion, ½ medium carrot, 2-3 inch celery stalk and 2-3 garlic cloves. Place in a pan with 1 bay leaf, 5-6 peppercorns, 2-3 cloves and 5 cups of water and bring to a boil. Lower heat and simmer for 15 minutes and strain. Cool and store in a refrigerator till further use.

- *Wonton Wrappers*

  Knead 2 cups of refined flour with ½ cup warm water to make a firm dough. Roll the dough into a large thin square sheet, about 1 mm thick. Cut into 3-inch squares and use as required.

Glossary

ENGLISH	HINDI
Asafoetida	Hing
Basil	Tulsi
Bottle gourd	Lauki
Button mushrooms	Khumb
Cloves	Laung
Cottage cheese	Paneer
Cumin seeds	Jeera
Gram, green skinless split	Dhuli moong dal
Gram, green split	Chilkewali moong dal
Gram, whole green	Sabut moong
Lemon grass	Chai ki patti

ENGLISH	HINDI
Lettuce	Salad ke patte
Musk Melon	Kharbooj
Mustard	Rai
Olives	Jaitun
Red pumpkin	Kaddu
Refined flour	Maida
Spinach	Palak
Split pigeon peas	Toovar dal/ Arhar dal
Spring onion	Hara pyaaz
Vinegar	Sirka
Walnuts	Akhrot